FREEDOM
WITH
ALTITUDE

Breaking The Mold And
Creating An Unstoppable
Mindset In Times Of
Uncertainty

Andre Vicario

Table of Contents

Introduction

The purpose of my book is to share both my good and bad life experiences to help others realize they can strive for more. In this world, we are penalized or admonished for doing well. We are missing the point. We all have the same ability in a 24-hour period to make choices. Those choices determine the quality of our life.

I wanted more out of life. In doing so, I went to hell and back multiple times along the way. Some of those bad experiences were self-induced, but I am where I am today because of ALL my life experiences.

How do you measure your success... money, possessions, recognition, feelings, or personal fulfillment? You don't have to choose just one. It can be a combination. Whichever it is for you, do you feel successful? If you do, congratulations. If not, what is preventing you from living the life you anticipated. Most fall under the latter and live their lives hoping things will change or miraculously fall into a pool of money.

The most important takeaway from this book is *change*. Change constantly occurs. You are either on one side or the other. You must change your course with intent, or it will change you. Personally, I like to control change and guide the navigation to my destination of choice. Many want change but expect it without doing anything different. That doesn't work.

As you read my book, nothing in my background would indicate my life turning out the way it has. I have felt inadequate from the beginning and learned to use this as an asset versus a liability. Impressing myself was a much bigger win than impressing others.

If you are looking to change the direction of your life course, this book will give you some essential tools to do so. It will share the challenges we face and how perseverance combined with a relentless attitude will set you free. We all have demons in the back of our heads, continuously reminding us we are not good enough. The book will help you recognize these patterns to allow a new outcome to occur. You will be inspired to heavily evaluate who you surround yourself with because of the direct impact on your success and happiness. This book is also for those who doubt themselves and those who feel they deserve more. It will help you understand, you deserve exactly what you get, good or bad. We are where we are as a result of our choices, not the challenges we face. There aren't any shortcuts in this book, rather a story of sheer fortitude combined with a relentless resolve to live a life without limitations or restrictions. A life by design, not default.

To Your Success,

Andre

CHAPTER 1

THE AMERICAN DREAM?

Chapter 1:
The American Dream?

Nothing about my childhood pointed to me one day becoming a multimillionaire, but I did. It wasn't a miracle that brought me here; it has been my mindset cultivated over time and often through the fire of seemingly insurmountable obstacles. I have literally spent my life giving people the tools to create their own American Dream. I can tell you, after over two decades of being on the frontlines of the financial industry, the single most significant factor separating the rich and poor is the difference in mindset. This book is dedicated to laying out the key mindset markers that will keep you stuck or set you free.

America is the wealthiest country in the world and also carries the most significant wealth gap. Why are so many people feeling trapped, struggling from paycheck to paycheck, and then retiring with barely enough to stay afloat or, worse, unable to retire at all? There is a crisis in the financial mind of everyday America. Whether the proverbial system works or doesn't, this can no longer serve as an excuse to live a financially distressed life. Over 50% of U.S. people age 65 or older have a median savings of $150,000 to last what might be a 30-year retirement. Doing the math, this breaks down to about $5,000 per year, explaining why the largest growing working population is over 65, and retirement is nowhere in sight.

It doesn't have to stay this way, but people struggle to see a way forward.

This crisis is a symptom stemming from the epidemic of a profound misunderstanding about our human potential and creating wealth that has crept into everyday American's hearts and minds. It's as if we have never fully recovered from the psychological shock and practical fallout from the 1929 Great Depression. Every new economic downturn sends people retreating even further back into the belief that money is scarce and can be gone in an instant. The Global pandemic of 2020 had people feeling more uncertain than ever about their present and future wellbeing.

People are asking if the American Dream is still alive? Has your confidence in yourself or your dreams been hit so hard it just doesn't feel possible to get back up again? In the chapters to follow, I want to show you the American Dream is not only alive but thriving and has never been more accessible than it is today with a few powerful shifts in your thinking.

Yes, even as we forge ahead through economic downturns.

What is your "American Dream"?

The American Dream is defined as *the ideal by which equality of opportunity is available to any American, allowing the highest aspirations and goals to be achieved.*

Notice the American Dream says nothing about it being easy or hard, passionate or mundane, fair or unfair; it's simply equality of opportunity available to reach your desired goals.

I'm a great example of what's possible because I grew up as a minority, with very little money or support and exactly zero handouts.

When we live in the wealthiest, opportunity-rich country in the world and over half of the population is barely getting by, it doesn't add up. It's outrageous.

I will make two bold statements, and at the end of the book, we will revisit them and see if your thoughts have changed at all by then.

1. There is no excuse to stay poor in America if you don't want to be.

2. You can change your financial situation whenever you decide you are going to change it.

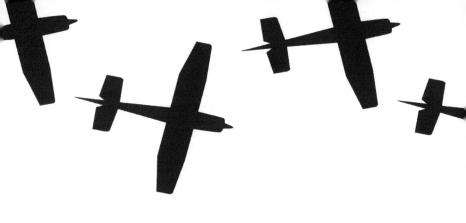

NO ONE COULD DETERMINE MY SUCCESS OR FAILURE BUT ME.

Andre Vicario

I don't sit in the cheap seats in any area of life. My voice is hard-won from coming face to face every day with what's possible in life, business for myself, and helping others get ahead. I have challenged every part of myself that scares me, and I know the gut wrench of losing and the exhilaration of winning. I have played full out since I was a kid.

I am living proof that the American Dream is there for the taking to any man, woman, or child who decides they want to build more for themselves, their families, and others.

I know this because I started with nothing. Today, I have more than I ever imagined. I broke out of a mold that could have easily and without question sentenced me to a life of personal and financial struggle. Following every battle, I gained altitude, and the more I rose, the freer I became.

I didn't even know what the American Dream was. I was a young kid who was taught from day one we don't have enough money, period. My job was to put my head down, work hard, and be grateful for the roof above and the food on the table, which I was. There was never talk of, "someday if I worked hard, I could create anything I could fathom."

I was cast into a mold that was made of fear, scarcity, and insecurity. We didn't have enough, and I certainly didn't feel like I was enough. If I took the advice given, my best bet for survival in this world was to work as hard as possible, don't rock the boat, and just pray that I work hard enough to keep the lights on and food on the table. As long as the bottom line was taken care of each month, that was the best we could hope. If something better than that happened then, it was luck, and it would have to fall out of the sky. This was not the American Dream I had in mind.

My parents meant well; they taught me what they had been taught about money and life. They, too, had been cast into a mold of fear, scarcity, and insecurity by the generations before them. My parents loved me but wanted me to understand that life was hard, making money was even harder, and making a lot of money was next to impossible. They wanted to make sure I would never go hungry and would be able to keep my lights on in a modest little house someday, so I needed to understand that I was going to need to work very, very hard for the rest of my life to make ends meet as they had. It's not that they didn't want more for my siblings or me; they just didn't believe that more was possible. Where you get your advice from is paramount when it comes to wealth and success. My parents' advice came from a place of love and their desire to help me not fail, but it did not help guide me out of a poor mindset.

No one sat down with my parents, or their parents, or their parents and explained how to create wealth in America and the mindset and rules required to make it happen. They had no idea, and they did the very best they could with every bit of what they knew to do. My parents had been shown how to take care of food and shelter, month to month, and work hard every day without question.

This never resonated with me.

Working every day as hard as you can just to break even didn't make sense to me. I was so confused. I had no problem working hard but working hard to barely get by just didn't seem right. I was alone in questioning the validity of the strategies for life around me.

I found myself questioning the status quo from an early age. I had always felt out of place like a black sheep in my family.

Early on, something had happened that may have created my greatest weakness and, simultaneously, my greatest strength.

I felt like I was a mistake.

I was the youngest of four and a complete accident. I use the word mistake because that was the word used growing up when talking about my conception. From this, I carried a feeling of inadequacy. It messed with me. I was confused about many things as a kid, but the uncertainty I felt about my place in this world was unrivaled by the rest of what went through my head. It came up often throughout my youth that I was the great "oops."

I don't think it was ever meant to hurt me, but it got in my head and stayed with me for decades. Something in me became relentlessly driven to prove that I deserve to be here, that I am enough, and that I am not a mistake. As much turmoil as this has caused me inside, it drove me to look at life differently, question things that maybe I wouldn't have, and find a way to create a different path. I wanted to prove to myself and my family that I belong here. I spent most of my life trying to silence the voice of inadequacy that repeatedly whispered in the backdrop of everything I did.

Back then, I just seemed rebellious in the way I thought differently about things and questioned everything. I may have even seemed arrogant, but I can assure you I had created the shield to protect the uncertainty I felt on the inside. I don't think I or anyone else knew exactly where it was coming from. I just knew I wanted more out of life than what I saw around me, and I didn't know how I would do it or what it would take, but I was determined to find a way somehow.

This was solidified when I was exposed to other families doing life differently. I would consider those my first mentors. They worked hard but seemed to have a lot more financial independence, free time, a nice home, and did fun things. Paying attention to other people doing life differently from my family heavily influenced me by elevating what I thought might be possible. They were living like I wanted to live someday, I knew I just needed to learn whatever they knew, and then I could take the actions that would get me to a better place in life.

I had my father's work ethic coupled with my own drive and vision for more; no one could determine my success or failure but me. Despite my constant feelings of inadequacy breathing down my back, I just focused on moving forward. I didn't understand until later in my life just how crucial my mindset was to success. I learned many brutal lessons the hard way, but I was teachable, and my mindset has taken me places that I didn't think were possible.

MINDSET HAS TAKEN ME PLACES THAT
I DIDN'T THINK WERE POSSIBLE.

===

Andre Vicario

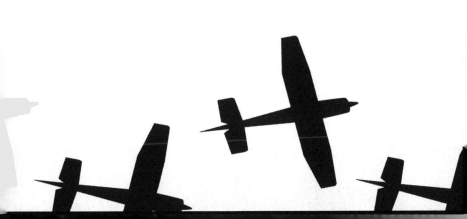

Today, my wife and I have built a continually expanding investment firm, ModFinancial "Where Dreams Take Flight" (formerly CalChoice Financial), bringing financial independence to thousands of people and their families every day. My purpose is to help people have a better financial life; individually, I can only meet and help so many people. Building a company with the same purpose-minded individuals will allow us to change this generation and many generations to follow. When people work with my company, they can be assured a great experience by selfless advisors who share this purpose, making the financial lives of the clients we serve. I have a team that I could not be more proud of or grateful for that show up invariably to make a difference in this world, creating custom blueprints for people to break free from financial struggle and pull their American dream into reality.

I personally have complete financial freedom, have retired my parents, and get to take our family, friends, or team anywhere at any time in jets that I own and some I fly myself.

I'm sharing this with you not to impress you but rather impress upon you the possibilities that lie ahead when you decide to go after what you want. I know it's possible to make it happen despite any perceived obstacle you may have.

I did it:

Starting with nothing

Knowing nothing

As a minority

With a young wife and baby just after highschool

Feeling completely inadequate

Not knowing how

Overcoming significant despair from ruthless learning curves

And I ran into massive obstacles along the way.

I did it and am doing it every day still.

And you can too.

I have failed many times, which developed the character equity that gives me the confidence to keep going. I learned from the failures and turned them into a positive as I will not make the same mistakes. I'm not implying you need to take the same path I have to gain freedom, but if you apply the mindset shifts that I have used to create a successful path outlined in this book, you will be well on your way.

I have dedicated my entire career to acquiring every resource necessary to give people what my family needed way back when; the right knowledge, advice, and investment opportunities that would have changed their lives forever.

Now, I want to show people how I took myself from the kid who felt like a mistake with no money to the man who has dreams come to life daily. I want you to have the freedom I have if you want it. I want to help you stop dreaming about the American Dream and get the mindset and direction you need to actually do it.

CHAPTER 2

THE "POOR" MINDSET

Chapter 2:
The "Poor" Mindset

Being poor is a mindset; being broke is a temporary circumstance. Some people define being poor as not having money. I define being poor as continually being worried there is not enough money. When you're broke, you might technically not have cash available, but you know you can get more. You have resources, even the character mental equity, to find it. I have had money tied up in various ventures before and could have been considered broke, but I wasn't poor because it never crossed my mind that I couldn't make more money. When Elon Musk sold PayPal for $180 million and two weeks later was borrowing money for rent after reinvesting his money into other companies, was he now poor? No, he was temporarily broke, strategically broke. When you have a financial plan that you know you can successfully execute and know where your money is coming from and where it's going— you stop worrying because you know exactly where you are heading. If you are worried sick about money and no matter how much you make, you believe there's never enough, you are poor.

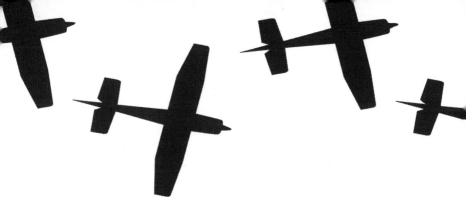

BEING POOR IS A MINDSET; BEING BROKE
IS A TEMPORARY CIRCUMSTANCE.

==

Andre Vicario

There are plenty of people that have money in their bank account, and they are living paycheck to paycheck with no clear way to retire. They believe there will never be enough money and their actions reflect this belief, leaving them feeling trapped. Being poor is a mental state. It's not just worrying about money; it's the lack of belief you can earn more or create the opportunity to earn more. Being poor is a choice, as is being wealthy. They both take effort. One takes effort and sacrifice, and the other takes effort to choose to do nothing. Both are decisions. The choice is yours, take action and fail but learn and do it again or don't take any action and be a victim to this mindset. Being poor is not always about having enough money; it's more along the lines of thought process. You may not have a lot of money or any money, but how you think will determine if you're poor or broke. Money is a measuring tool but not always indicative of the situation. Not having a lot of money does not mean you are poor if you are happy and content with your situation. See, it's truly about mindset. If you want, you can have. You must know there are sacrifices and commitments necessary to change your situation. Ask yourself what makes you happy, what inspires you? Turn your passions into a noble purpose, and you can feel as wealthy as a billionaire because you are happy and in a great place doing what you are passionate about and making a difference.

If you currently feel trapped, no amount of worrying will directly change your situation. It's time to take action. Write out all of your financial obligations and add them up in comparison to what you are taking home from income. This is the best place to start; clarifying your current bottom line will allow you to identify shortfalls and perhaps unnecessary shortfalls. Taking this fundamental action can lead you to precisely where you need to take action, either reduce spending or find an additional source of income. It's a sacrifice and a commitment that we will talk about in later chapters, but first, we have to address what's going on in your head.

There is a reason why hard work doesn't always equal financial independence. Certain beliefs create a "poor mindset." Suppose you want to change your economic trajectory away from the poor mindset. In that case, these are the primary limiting beliefs you must shift to move ahead differently for yourself and your family.

Beliefs that make you poor with or without money:

1. *My financial situation is out of my control.*

Many things in life are out of your control, the weather, and other people, to name a couple, but your financial independence is 100% within your control. The minute you believe that something outside of yourself has circumstantially taken control of your ability to create wealth, then you have handed over your power. No one takes away your mind, your choices, and the actions you take. If you can learn, make choices, and take steps based on what you learn, you have the most foundational elements required to build a new path for yourself. You would be shocked by how many people make the same choices leading to the same mistakes repeatedly without learning and doing it differently. If you have lost your job, can't find a job, lost an investment, closed a business, or some other kind of hardship has come your way- you are still in control of your financial independence. You get to choose to keep going, exhaust every resource to learn the information you need, to take the kind of actions necessary to get yourself into a different place. How you respond is entirely up to you. Identify with someone you feel is where you want to be and talk with them about their journey. A mentor or advisor is another place to start. Opportunities are all around us every day, but we don't always know how to recognize them. Having discussions with successful people will help you in identifying opportunities you may not recognize. If an advisor gave you this book, then you know someone personally that can help you right now.

2. *It's someone else's fault that I am in the position I'm in.*

Blame is similar to the first Poor Mindset belief that your financial situation is out of your control but takes it a step further into *deciding who or what is in control if not you.* Believing that something or someone other than you is in charge of your outcomes can create a lifetime of distraction that self-justifies staying stuck and feeling victimized. When you feel like your financial wellbeing is out of your control, it can render you powerless in your own eyes. Further, when you target someone or something as the cause of your financial struggle, it's game over—waiting for someone to come and save you evokes a sense of powerlessness. You need to save yourself. If your car was totaled by someone who had no insurance and it wasn't your fault, and no one offered to fix your car, would you then decide to walk for the rest of your life, or would you get your car fixed or get a new car? It may not have been your fault that your car was damaged, but if no one will fix it, how long would you choose to be car-less? The truth is we save ourselves, and ideally, we do our very best to help others in the process. There is a point when blame must stop being used as an agent to justify inaction. How often do you hear people say they had a successful business until they got screwed or the government changed things? They don't ever want to say, "I had a great business, but I messed it up and lost it." They will forever let this linger and dictate how they communicate with others from a victim's perspective. Once we accept our failures, we begin to grow as we learn from them. You have to take responsibility and take action to move everything in your life forward. People always want to place blame vs. taking responsibility for things not working out as intended. Ironically, taking ownership of the failure and understanding why it happened is the primary way to ensure it doesn't happen again.

3. *I don't know what to do, so I'll keep doing what I've been doing.*

We all know the old adage about insanity; doing the same thing again repeatedly, expecting a different outcome has never worked. If you aren't where you want to be financially, you can't afford not to learn new information to get you on a path toward your goals. Whatever you've been doing got you exactly where you are now. This is why working hard does not always mean financial independence. If you have been working hard and still feel stuck, then there is a serious problem, and something has to change. Of course, keep doing what *is* working, but it's time to upgrade your information in any area that's not working. You need to seek out and apply new knowledge actively. The poor mindset doesn't believe learning new information will help change their problems with money. One of the best ways to follow in the steps of the wealthy is to find mentors to teach you proven financial strategies that will help you.

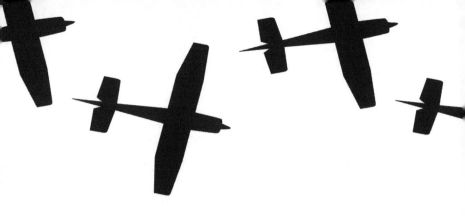

WHATEVER YOU'VE BEEN DOING GOT
YOU EXACTLY WHERE YOU ARE NOW.

===

Andre Vicario

4. *I don't have enough money to get ahead.*

The actions or inactions we take today are tomorrow's results. One of the biggest tickets to getting away from living paycheck to paycheck without any money growing for your future is a willingness to start now right where you are. I guarantee you can carve out some portion of your income, no matter how small, to put aside and invest in your future. The money grows, and your ability to make more and invest more begins to grow when you commit to the mindset that you can and must start with wherever you're at today. Every time you tell yourself you can't begin to make changes with where you are today is the exact moment you choose to stay the same. Change is an essential part of growth, and knowledge will set you free. What books have you read, and who are the people you listen to?

Scarcity comes from the fear that there's not enough. The scarcity mindset is synonymous with a poor mindset. We have all heard the stories of people who have won the lottery only to find themselves back to where they were financially in a few short years. When you believe there isn't enough, the actions follow, and you find this self-fulfilling prophecy to be true. There is absolutely no shortage of opportunity or money in this world. The truth is we all have the ability to create our opportunities and make our own money. When you begin to sincerely look for how to make more money, generate more wealth, etc., you will find it everywhere.

I had a turbulent beginning the first time I had to start making real money. When I first started, the only thing

I knew for sure is that I would figure it out. My wife Kim and I found out we were having a baby, and we were kids having a kid at barely 20. She was in college in one state, and I was in college in another, and I thought I had time to figure out what I wanted to do with my life. Suddenly everything changed on a dime. We were young and had no clue how we were going to make it all work. I needed a job right away, and I had played football in school, so I applied at a local gym and began working as a personal trainer. I quickly learned the ropes and made enough to cover our bottomline, but we were nowhere near comfortable. When the gym owner came to me and asked if I'd be interested in buying the gym, I jumped at the opportunity. I was resourceful and found the money to make it happen; the only problem, I knew nothing about owning or running a business. I give myself credit for having the guts to jump in and go for it, but one of my greatest mistakes I learned from this experience was how vital asking for advice is to success. I was still at a point in my life where I thought I needed to act like I knew everything, and asking for help meant I was somehow weak. Looking back, I know that my insecurities played a dominant role in my refusal of mentorship in that venture, and it almost cost me everything.

I had a poor mindset and didn't know it. I began making excellent money at the gym and, before long, acquired three more gyms. All four gyms were turning a substantial profit, and I had never had money before, and I had a lot to prove. I began spending money like crazy. I bought Kim and me new nice cars, new everything. I blew money on every friend I had, dinners, drinks, and God only knows. For five years, the more I made, the more I spent, never stopping to ask for help. Everything was spinning out of control and bottoming out. Everything was falling apart around me, including but not limited to having to file bankruptcy. Kim gave me an ultimatum, family or this crazy situation I had created. I chose family and a new direction as Kim and I are happily celebrating over three decades together but, back then, things had become highly turbulent with no clean landing in sight. I sold everything and scarcely made it out. I felt so depressed and defeated that I parked myself by my parents' pool for six months and watched the O.J. Simpson trial (not my proudest moment), but I had no idea what to do next. Eventually, I knew it was time for me to get back on the horse but differently than before.

I had two choices; get a job that really supports my family to create financial independence or die trying. I had always been interested in being a stockbroker; mind you, this was during the time when Wall Street had hit the theaters and made being a stockbroker very sexy, but I wasn't sure what I wanted. I showed up to an interview to become a financial advisor, and the man who interviewed me decided to take a chance to bring me aboard. Today, all these years later, the man who gave me my start in the industry heads one of my departments, and I will always be grateful.

I did a deep dive into the world of finance and made the decision I would do anything and everything necessary to create stability for my family. I didn't wait for anyone to tell me I could do it. I didn't hope something would come my way. I took every action possible to move us ahead, and when I was stuck, I exhausted every resource to get unstuck. I made a decision not to be poor. If one thing fell through, sometimes everything would fall through. I would persevere until I found what would work. I could deal with being broke, but I would never have a poor mindset again.

I did work hard, but I looked for ways to do it smarter. I was still reeling from the bankruptcy and my year of what felt like depression, but I had to move forward. I asked questions and made connections intentionally everywhere I went with the purpose of learning and creating opportunities.

In my mind, there was always more, more opportunity, more ways to figure something out, more questions I could ask to get me to the next step, more calls I could make that could connect me with a new opportunity to move us in the right direction. Believing there is always more, is abundance. The abundance mindset is the antidote to the scarcity or poor mindset.

When you understand there is an unlimited supply of doors to open in this world, you stop wasting your time staring at the ones that get closed and keep moving.

Chapter 2: Reflect

List 5 opportunities you have right now that could increase your income.

_____

_____

_____

_____

_____

Now list one action you could take in the next 24 hours to make each opportunity happen.

_____

_____

_____

_____

_____

_____

CHAPTER 3

THE FRIENDS YOU KEEP

Chapter 3:
The Friends You Keep

Reality is reinforced by groups of people who share similar values, thoughts, and beliefs. It's no secret that who we spend our time with heavily influences what we think and feel about life and the world in which we live. Growing up, I was surrounded by people who saw money as hard to make. Working hard was a way to make ends meet each month, not as a way to create financial independence. Financial independence was not discussed, let alone how to make it happen. I was influenced by people who had been surrounded by others their whole lives with so many perceived limitations about what was possible for themselves. These perceived limitations were molded and solidified each day by how they talked and the actions they took.

No one questioned the absurdity of working so hard, only to have to say every weekend, "Sorry, we can't, we just don't have the money." The people we surround ourselves with create the climate we adjust to. Why would we question what no one around us is questioning? If the people around us aren't alarmed by the fact that money is always tight and every month is stressful in terms of keeping the bills paid, then it would be natural for us to surrender our dreams and accept life the way it is...

THE PEOPLE WE SURROUND OURSELVES WITH CREATE
THE CLIMATE WE ADJUST TO.

==

Andre Vicario

You don't bring big dreams around small thinkers.

What happens when one person begins to question the way things have always been done in a group? Commonly, the person is met with resistance in the form of ridicule or defensiveness. We all have a need to justify our actions and why we do what we do. Most of the time, we don't even know why we do what we do, so we just make things up without realizing it. If you want to uncover when you or someone else has no idea why they are doing what they are doing, look for answers like these:

Because I said so.

Because that's how life works.

Because that's the way it has always been.

Because that's how our family does it.

Because that's what people do.

When you press in on these answers with further questions of "why?" it tends to trigger anger and frustration. No one likes to have the world they understand get shaken even when you're trying to help. Let's follow this thread for a second.

Person A: "Why do you work so hard but never seem to get ahead?"

Person B: "Because that's how life works."

Person A: "What do you mean? Why do you think that?"

Person B: "Because that's how it's always been."

Person A: "Why don't you change it?"

Person B: "I've tried. I can't. It's just the way life is. It's fine. We are hard workers. That's how we do it in this family."

Person A: "I think it can be different. Some people work hard and make significant money."

Person B: "Well, good for them, I wasn't born with a silver spoon in my mouth and haven't had anything handed to me. I'm proud of the hard work I do and the roof over our head that I provide."

Person A: "Yes, what you have done is great, but what if you could learn how to create more wealth so your hard work could make you a lot more money and someday you wouldn't have to work so hard."

Person B: "Ok, that's enough of you criticizing me."

Person A: "I'm not criticizing you. I'm honestly asking if you want to know more information that could help you get ahead and not worry about money so much?"

Person B: "All right, that's enough. I'm not a lazy person who thinks there is an easy road in this world. I'm done talking about this."

Person A: "I don't understand. I am just trying to help. Why does the conversation have to stop?"

Person B: "Because I said so."

You might relate to this somehow, trying to help someone who needs help but doesn't want help. It's hard on everybody. Being open to new information is such an essential part of success and financial independence regardless of industry.

The most intelligent people know they don't know everything. If you want to go beyond the place you're currently in, you, without question, will need new information to go on. If you already knew what to do, you would have done it. There was a time early on where I thought asking for help felt like weakness, as I've mentioned, but I can say nearly three decades in, that exposing yourself to the correct information and mindset is a cornerstone to breaking the mold of living with a poverty mindset. Believing that somehow we should just innately know everything is so irrational when you think about it. The only way we learn is to ask questions of the right people, in books, in podcasts, in training workshops, etc.

For those of you that have children as I do, I'm sure you've experienced those times where your child was struggling to do something new but simultaneously didn't want help because they were confident they already knew what to do. You could see their frustration, and you knew exactly what to do, and if they would just let you help them, you knew you could save them the pain of the struggle. I used to think I needed to do everything myself. My early life lessons from watching my family struggle and spending time with some family friends who weren't struggling sent the message loud and clear that I needed to know new information. I wasn't going to get it without seeking it out.

I realized something significant that I have carried with me since "you don't ask for advice from people who don't live the life you want to live." If you are searching for a way to move to the next level in your life and learn how to create financial independence— you do not ask your broke, struggling family member or friend for their input on how. If you dream of traveling the world, you don't look for support and guidance from someone who has never left their hometown. If you want to know how the wealthy do it, find a person willing to share how they did it. Find someone you respect and admire who has the lifestyle you would like, ask questions and learn from them. Sometimes it may just be the positivity you need, or they may have the guidance you are looking for. Surround yourself with this environment daily until you exude this mindset of possibility. Sometimes it's even the person you share a bed with who is holding you back. They may not intentionally do this, but change can be frightening for some people. Listen to how people respond to your dreams or ideas, you will now be consciously listening for negativity or bad advice based on things this person doesn't know. Time and time again, families and friends will sit and talk about their dreams and ideas and regurgitate the same pre-conditioned limitations they've always perceived. Instead of having a genuine conversation about what's possible and how to achieve it, the conversation becomes a support group reaffirming why it's ok that it's never going to happen. I am not saying to be successful, you need to leave your friends and loved ones behind, but you need to make new friends if you feel stuck.

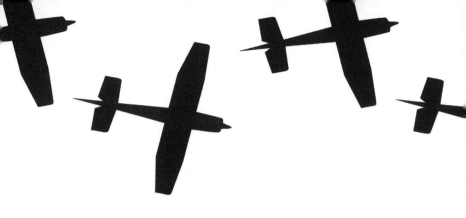

YOU DON'T BRING BIG DREAMS AROUND SMALL THINKERS.

Andre Vicario

The late motivational speaker Jim Rohn said, "You are the average of the five people you spend the most time with." Give this some serious thought and ask yourself if these people are who you want to become and are they living the life you want to live?

Don't panic if you realize the answer is no, for some, even a hell no. This doesn't mean you don't love or respect them, and it doesn't mean you have to cut them off, but as I said before, you must actively expose yourself to the people you want to be like. If you don't know anyone personally, it's okay; the people you can learn from by reading their book, listening to their podcasts, joining their groups, watching them on their Youtube channels, or hiring their advisors are endless. You have to do whatever you must to open a new gateway of new information coming into your mind and world, or you will stay exactly where you are. The great news is you have already begun; reading this book can be a catalyst of change for you.

Find a mentor yesterday. A mentor is even better than a friend because you know you have come to learn, and they know they have come to teach. Relationships built on intentional growth are by far the most transformational. I have had many mentors, and to be honest, I love, hated my best mentor. I learned some of my greatest lessons from him, mostly what not to do, which is invaluable. He pushed me to my breaking point some days and pissed me off like no one else on occasion. He also helped me rise to a potential I wasn't sure I had in me. His expectations of me were so high that it forced me to rise well beyond my personal highest expectations for myself. I went from good to great working with that son of a gun. I may be self-made, but you never do anything extraordinary alone.

How do you know you have found the right person or group of people?

Today, I surround myself with people who are either living the aspirations that I have or have a growth mindset.

You know you're on the right track if you can check the following off the list when seeking out your sphere of influence or tribe:

*They challenge the limitations you feel like you have in reaching your goals with solutions.

*They carry the traits you aspire to develop in yourself.

*Their goals are as big as if not bigger than yours.

*They practice what they preach.

*When you are around them or exposed to their work, they make you want to be a better person.

*They are purpose-driven.

*They focus on possibility and solutions.

You know you are off track if the following describes the people you choose to spend your time with:

* Being around them makes you feel ok about being stuck.

*They agree with nearly everything you say.

* They talk more about the past than they do about the future.

* They have the same struggles as you.

* If they snapped their fingers and could give you what they have, you wouldn't want it.

* They have expressed a goal for more than a year and have not followed through.

*They talk more about problems than they do solutions.

I have had to let go of some relationships throughout my life and as hard as change is, staying the same is much more challenging. The price of refusing to grow will be paid with handing over your dreams to stagnancy. The American Dream sits on the shelves of life, and if you dare to grow, it's yours for the taking.

You get to decide who you are and what you want to become at any age and who you do it with matters. You can not choose your family, but you can choose the ones you spend your time with.

Chapter 3: Reflect

Write down the top 5 people you spend the most time with:

_____

_____

_____

_____

_____

Are these people who you want to be like? If yes, how so?

_____

_____

_____

_____

_____

List 3 people you would like to be like and how you can spend more time with them.

Example: Coffee, lunch, listen to their podcast, or read their book.

_____

_____

_____

_____

_____

CHAPTER 4

THE EXCUSES WE MAKE

Chapter 4:

The Excuses We Make

My first instinct has often been to hit goals with brute internal force. If I sensed something that felt weak in me, I would out-perform it with equal and opposite intensity. When fear would rush in, I would get quiet then run even harder and faster at my goals. When I felt inadequate, I would exceed even my own expectations. I built a fortress of protection around my family and me, and it came in the form of success. I had every reason to back down from high expectations for myself. It was ingrained in me early that being Hispanic could be a disadvantage; further, I carried the belief that I wasn't good enough and did not deserve more.

I had not seen anyone in my immediate family become successful. Sometimes I felt guilty because I wanted more out of life. What if it meant that I thought I was "too good" for hard work, as my father would say. I knew I had no problem with hard work; I believed in the work ethic, but I also knew I needed to apply the principles differently. Becoming a young father and husband before I even had my feet on the ground was one of the most significant challenges I have faced. It was never an option for me to do the right thing for my new family, but this is when I realized being told what I was going to do, didn't work for me. It was an interesting time as Kim was Mormon and I was not. This was a pivotal time for me as I look back at my life. I remember Kim's father coming to my apartment and telling me I was going to marry her or she would be sent to Utah to raise my son in the Mormon church. I was not about to allow this or someone telling me what I was going to do. I don't know where I would be today if my now father-in-law didn't come to me with these demands. I realized then, I have control of my decisions and direction for my life. I cannot thank him enough for this experience, it changed my mental attitude in ways I will forever be grateful for.

What was a seemingly challenging time for us all turned out to be a great experience for us, and today we have the best relationship. Back then, the only advantage I had was my mindset. I had no money and no experience starting out, and everything I had seen and heard told me having more just wasn't in the cards for me. Despite all of this, I believed I had the ability to create my own destiny. Something deep inside of me knew I get to decide how my life turns out. That was my winning hand. I decided there would never be an excuse for me to accomplish anything less than my goals in life. Notice I use the word excuse instead of reason. Reason implies a justified explanation for an action or event. Excuse implies an off-load of responsibility to justify an action or an event.

Here is an example of the difference between excuse and reason.

"I didn't get the milk at the store because I had a flat tire."

Some might see this as a reason for not getting the milk. Understandably, there is no milk due to the flat tire.

Some might see this as an excuse. I understand that getting a flat tire changed the plan for attaining the milk, but there are many other ways to get the milk.

Obviously, the milk isn't a big deal, but this exemplifies the mindset of reasons versus excuses.

By reason and logic, it would have been understandable for me to struggle through life. But to me, those reasons were excuses. If I stayed stuck, I could have blamed it on my past, circumstances, and lack of experience, but I refused because I knew I ultimately decided my life's outcome by my actions. At my core, I knew those were excuses, ways for me to attempt to sidestep my responsibility in my own life.

This might ruffle a few feathers and if you recall from our last chapter, challenging our own perceived limitations is critical for growth. I would start practicing now by staying open.

If you look back and change the word reason to excuse when explaining what lead you to where you are today, you might be tempted to get defensive or beat yourself up--don't. We don't know what we don't know, and taking a high level of responsibility will only empower you to make extraordinary changes in your life moving forward. This is part of learning. I believe the main reason we fight learning a new way to do something is not that we have a problem with education; we are afraid to make mistakes. Looking back and realizing you made mistakes only sets you up for success if you can learn from them. It's only those who refuse to learn that indeed fail. It's part of success to get out there, do your best, do it wrong, fail, learn how to do it right, and eventually kick ass. The people who get out there, do their best, do it wrong, fail, refuse to learn anything new, and fail again could turn it around the second they decided to learn more. There is just no excuse for living a low-quality life if you don't want to.

If you want to get pro-active right now, do this exercise:

Write down a list of your perceived most significant failures with the sole purpose of discovering what you learned or what you could have done differently. This begins the learning process.

Decide if there is anything on the list you feel you gave up on but still want to make happen. Now you can go after it with a fresh perspective and a can-do mindset. Once you identify what it is, write out how it will end and work backward to where you are now. Beginning with the end in mind can help you with your steps to get it done this time. But first, you must decide if you really want it and are committed to seeing it through.

If yes, set time aside to learn more about the topic or goal from someone who has proven success in that specifically. To this day, I do a weekly introspection of my week. I know when I am justifying to myself and will quickly understand what needs to be done. By doing this, it forces me to view my week and determine if it was progressive and productive. If not, I know what will change the following week.

I guarantee you will learn what you needed to know the first time to succeed the next time.

I learned to fly a plane and have my pilot's license. This was a goal I had, to own my own jets and be able to fly them. I am one of the busiest people I know. I work hard and play hard, and I can tell you for sure that I did not have time to learn to fly a plane nor time to get all of my flight time logged. I did not have the time, but *I made the time*. Getting up at 4 am to fly before going into the office in the morning was inconvenient, but it was important to me and today is one of my most fulfilling achievements. It took me two years to receive my license because the first plane I was told I had to learn on was a 1958 Piper 130. It was a dinosaur. I knew I would never fly that kind of plane post-license, and I argued that I wanted to learn on a plane I actually liked flying. This drug out the timetable, but eventually, I was able to get my license flying a Cirrus, a plane that I enjoy flying. I can have breakfast in one state, a meeting in another, and be home for dinner seamlessly.

We make time for what we prioritize. Here is something interesting, I decided to get my pilot's license when I could not fly with our dog on a commercial flight. We were told she was too big, and I couldn't accept that limitation. I wanted Kim and me to be able to take her anywhere, and now we can. We have even begun a foundation to help animals in need called Hennessy Dog Foundation. My point, I could have easily accepted the reason I was unable to fly our dogs was because the commercial airlines forbid it, and no one would have blamed me, but I saw it as an excuse on my part. I knew if I had my pilot's license and my own planes, then I could make sure it never happened again.

WE MAKE TIME FOR WHAT WE PRIORITIZE.

===

Andre Vicario

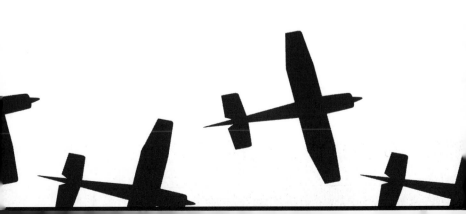

It's simple, if I don't take action toward the goals I set, then I can't call them goals. A life without excuses will hold you accountable to your own word. Have you ever had a goal but didn't tell anyone because you would feel accountable to see it through? Yes, everyone who is honest has done this. However, it turns out breaking our word to ourselves has an enormous impact on our self-confidence. Even when we don't tell a soul what our goals are, we know if we are following through or not. "Reasons" for not hitting your goals will pacify the warrior in you who needs and wants to make you proud. Decide up front that your reasons for not hitting your goals are excuses, and it can wake you up and set you free from holding yourself to a standard that consistently leaves you feeling like half the person you want to be. I like to talk about my goals to everyone until they become my reality. It forces me to get it done. I didn't like the feeling I would get when someone would ask me about a goal I mentioned, and it hadn't happened yet.

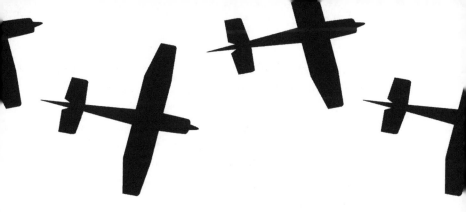

BREAKING OUR WORD TO OURSELVES HAS AN ENORMOUS
IMPACT ON OUR SELF-CONFIDENCE.

==

Andre Vicario

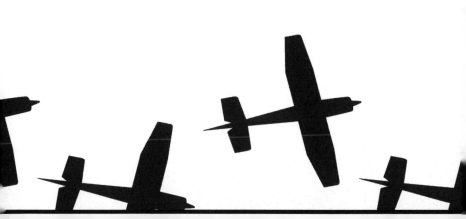

Chapter 4: Reflect

What are three goals you have wanted to set but not told anyone?

_____

_____

_____

_____

Choose one goal from those three that you want to achieve the most.

Set the date you will achieve the goal by.

Make time in your schedule to achieve the goal.

Tell someone you respect about your goal and your completion date. Telling others holds you accountable.

CHAPTER 5

EXPAND YOUR VISION

Chapter 5:
Expand Your Vision

Our lives reflect what we believe is possible. Our vision, our ability to think about and plan for the future using our imagination, is often what defines the parameters of possibility in our lives. If you are given a blank canvas and asked to draw your dream life, you might let your imagination run free. You might draw a dream life unrestrained by any of your perceived limitations about having that life. Now, if someone handed you a blank canvas and asked you to draw your dream life that *you believe you can achieve,* it might look completely different. Being able to imagine a great life usually isn't the problem. The problem comes when you realize you *don't believe* a dream life is possible for you. Our limiting beliefs harden around the edges of our lives. The beliefs you hold about money and life show up and draw a line in the sand separating what's possible for others and what's possible for you. We create our own limitations and restrictions, usually based on our past experiences and lessons from people who have not accomplished what they anticipated. Think of a child for a moment, they believe everything is possible until they hear otherwise. Isn't this totally unfortunate? We limit their beliefs in what is possible and what is not by how we suppress their minds and create restrictive barriers around them.

NO MATTER WHAT YOUR PAST HAS TOLD YOU ABOUT
WHO YOU ARE OR YOUR WORTH, YOU HAVE THE FINAL SAY.
===

Andre Vicario

Years ago I wanted to buy a nice boat. I was walking through the sales floor and already knew the boat I wanted. I had already done the research, knew I could afford the boat, and it was perfect. I spotted the model I was interested in and walked up to it, ready to take a look inside. The sales representatives were talking amongst themselves when I approached with my sister and wife, Kim. They brushed me aside, motioning they were busy, and even asked me to step back from the boat. Apparently, to them, I didn't look like a potential buyer. I have more stories than I can recall like this where I was overlooked because of a judgment made on the color of my skin. This played right into the insecurity I had carried my whole life, that somehow I didn't belong.

I had the money, but I was quickly marginalized as not a serious buyer because of my brown skin and my age (I was only 27 at the time). I walked away from the boat but still wanted to go back to look inside. My sister adamantly opposed saying how they treated me was unacceptable, and there's no way I should buy a boat from them. As we continued walking, a gentleman stepped out in front of me and asked if I would like to take a look at the boat behind him. I recognized it instantly as one of the most superior boats on the market and positive it wasn't in my price range and respectfully let him know. He said, "How do you know you can't afford it? Did someone already tell you that you couldn't?" I said that I know because I just know. I never even looked at this boat because it was bigger than my current vision of what was possible for me. I hadn't even entertained the idea. The gentlemen explained, until we go through the process and see what's possible, I couldn't possibly know yet if I could afford it or not. He invited me to take a look inside and sit down and talk. It turns out, to my surprise, I could comfortably afford the boat, and I bought it. It took someone showing me what was possible and giving me the right information to expand my vision. I learned that day how important it is to get more information beyond any limitations we set on ourselves. That sales rep stayed with us through every customization and even invited us to come and see the day she "got her heartbeat," hearing the engine ignite for the first time. It was truly one of the best buying experiences I've had. If I had let the way those other sales reps treated me define me that day, I would have missed out entirely. No matter what your past has told you about who you are or your worth, you have the final say. This whole experience was a massive lesson for me, never say no until you have to. Explore the possibilities first, then decide. I immediately said no, then found out it was possible.

OUR SCOPE OF VISION GROWS AS WE EXPOSE OURSELVES TO MORE INFORMATION ABOUT WHAT'S POSSIBLE AND HOW TO GET THERE.

==

Andre Vicario

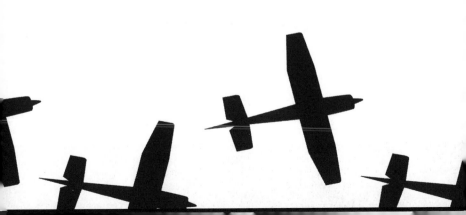

Our scope of vision grows as we expose ourselves to more information about what's possible and how to get there. Take the vantage points of a squirrel and an eagle. The squirrel can only see so much, and when it's making decisions about where to go and how much food is available, at best, it can climb to the top of a tree and look around. Apparently, squirrels travel about 5 miles a day and stay inside about 40 acres of land, slightly over half a square mile. Often when it's low to the ground, it can only see a short distance in front of it and is only familiar with the ground it has already covered. If you asked a squirrel to tell you about the world, it would do its best, but in truth, it may have only seen the forest it lives in.

The eagle, however, can cover 225 miles in a day and fly around 10,000 feet above the ground. An eagle can see something the size of a rabbit from 3 miles away. The vantage point of an eagle is far greater than that of a squirrel, so I imagine if you asked an eagle to tell you about the world, they could tell you a lot more than a squirrel.

Information is what expands the vantage point. Information is what allows you to expand your vision. The more information you have been exposed to from the people living the way you'd like to live, the greater your vision. When your vision is greater than the life you're currently living, and you have surrounded yourself with people who have big dreams themselves, you start crossing over the line of limitation you once had because you start believing it's possible for you too. If you were an eagle, surrounded by squirrels, and you asked them to tell you what your full potential is, can you imagine the misinformation? They would tell you, at best, you can see from the top of the highest tree and cover up to 5 miles a day by zig-zagging over the same 40 acres for the rest of your life. If you told them you'd like to instead cover 225 miles a day at 10,000 feet, they would think you were crazy. You wouldn't be inspiring. You would just sound nuts. But then, as the saying goes, first they all think you're crazy, and then everyone asks how you did it.

We rise to our vision for our lives and act based on what we believe is possible. Taking the same actions, listening to the same people, thinking the same thoughts day after day will keep you in the same place. There is nothing mind-blowing about this EXCEPT the fact that this happens every day on a mass scale, and people can't figure out why nothing is changing in their lives. Work, complain, stay the same, do it again the next day. This is the antithesis of wealth or abundance, and it only takes exposing yourself to new information and then applying the new knowledge for your life to change.

What if you don't know exactly what you want because you've never asked yourself with the sincerity of achieving it? That's fine, but now is the time to get clear on an expanded vision for your life.

Chapter 5: Reflect

Ask yourself these questions and answer them honestly:

1. How would you describe your thought process?
   Example: positive or negative, abundant or scarce?

   _____

   _____

   _____

   _____

2. Do people have a different perception of you
   than you do of yourself? If yes, describe both
   perceptions.

   _____

   _____

   _____

   _____

3. Who's perception is correct and why?

_____

_____

_____

_____

4. What is preventing you from taking the first step to a new elevated normal? Write down the obstacles and review them until you have a solution to eliminate them. There are always solutions. Do you have the commitment to follow through?

_____

_____

_____

_____

CHAPTER 6

==

HARD WORK DOESN'T GET YOU THERE

Chapter 6:

Hard work doesn't get you there.

Clarity of vision is the precursor to action that moves the needle to hit your goals. When you get clear on where you want to go, it's remarkable how much the desire to act increases. Nobody wants to run endlessly on a treadmill, and if we are going to put in the work, it needs to count and actually get you to a finish line that you want to cross. I think I've made it clear hard work is not the secret to success, considering how many people work hard and still feel stuck. *Strategic* hard work, however, creates a yellow brick road. Strategy works when you understand your end game. You can develop a plan of action that will get you your desired results. Working hard to execute your plan of action is motivating and makes sense. Working hard just to hit your self-made hard work quota is soul-crushing, in my opinion. People have asked me how I stay motivated and focused because I put in 16 hour days without even noticing and have for years. It's never been about putting in a 16 hour day; it's been about hitting the targets I set. When you wake up, and you know every action you take this day will produce a result that equals your dream life, it's motivating. I have things set up today where I can take time to vacation and do anything I can come up with, and everything keeps moving forward because I have an incredible team that grows by the day. In truth, I love working because the work I do is exactly what I want to be doing. Years ago, I wanted financial independence for my family and me. I was clear on my vision. I wanted to work in the world of finance and knew I had a lot to learn. Strategically I chose a field I was most interested in and learned what it would take for me to become the person who could run the companies I worked for. I set the goals and took every action necessary to get there. When I was 28 years old, I was the youngest managing director in the country, not just for the company I worked for but in the financial industry. I had interviewed for the company only two years prior, and I'll never forget getting promoted and given this vast office overlooking the Regent Beverly Wilshire in Beverly Hills. I had earned it by learning every square inch of the industry and doing my very best at all times. I worked very hard, but I knew exactly where it would take me. I recall feeling so excited yet entirely out of place. Those whispers of inadequacy in the back of my mind tried to slow me down, but I had a plan, and I stuck to it no matter what. When that company was bought out, I took a similar position with another company in Newport Beach, which was great, then I went into land banking to work with one of my mentors. My career in financial planning was soaring. I had created something stable and lucrative. This is where someone else might have relaxed a little, but I knew I was just getting started. I knew I wanted to help people on a bigger scale, and I knew there were areas in the financial industry that were not necessarily what was best for the client. I wanted to deliver options to people in a way that would 100% benefit them. I would need to create an investment firm that I could be proud of. I started CalChoice Investments in 2008 during the economic downturn. I was fortunate to have the ability to combine passion with purpose, this was the ultimate motivator, to serve others with a noble purpose and to improve the financial lives of the people around me. At first, it may have looked crazy, but this is what strategic action looks like. I knew it was the right move to help everyone if I was strong enough to see it through those turbulent times. I had learned everything I needed to create an investment firm that would truly serve people from all walks of life and change my family's lives for generations as well as the clients we served... I started CalChoice Financial (now ModFinancial) in 2015 as a result of a tarnished financial industry. This gave me purpose like I never had before, to disrupt an industry by actually serving your client's needs ahead of your own. This became my motivation and purpose for building this company. I want to be able to change this generation and the ones to follow by giving them access to the tools utilized by the wealthiest 1%.

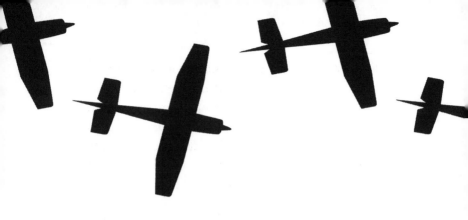

PASSION WITH PURPOSE IS THE ULTIMATE MOTIVATOR.

==

Andre Vicario

The hard work is only worth it inside of a clear strategy attached to a clear goal. The first two years of getting the company off the ground were hell. If it could go wrong, it did, Kim and I faced constant adversity. Had there not been a clear vision in place that we believed in and a strategic plan guiding us through what sometimes felt impossible, we wouldn't have made it.

I'll never forget coming home one day, and my son said there was a crazy letter taped to the door saying something about us needing to move out of our house and that it was a mistake. Kim and I never let our boys know how bad things were financially during those couple of years. I laughed it off and told him it was probably some crazy marketing scheme. I knew exactly what the letter was, a Notice of Default (NOD), and you get one right before your house is going into foreclosure. Kim and I used everything we had to start the company and sold everything we could to float it. We had to stop paying most of our bills to pay our team and overhead. Years prior, when I bought the first gym, I bought my parents' house and took out a second on their mortgage to pay for the acquisition and took over their house payments to retire them. When I received a NOD for my parents' home, it cut me to the bone. I had fully retired my parents by then, and I couldn't even fathom failing them by losing their home.

We stayed the course. Kim called me at the office after receiving a letter from the electric company stating our electricity was going to be shut off by 5:00 that day. I knew things were not going to change in the next two hours, so I asked her when was the last time we had a candlelight dinner, she was silent. I asked her to bring out some candles and let's have a family dinner in the candlelight. Fortunately, the electricity was not shut off, and we were able to pay it the next day.

There is always a perspective to take, the choice is yours. I was more than overwhelmed, but I kept growing the business, making calls, building our team, pushing forward, and a couple of contracts I had in escrow closed on the eleventh hour. Kim and I drove to the bank in Pasadena, California, with $78,632.00 to bring my parents home current practically 24 hours before the bank officially foreclosed on the property. We left the bank, had lunch, and I remember buying a pair of sunglasses to celebrate saving their home. As Kim and I drove home, we reset the clock because now we had 30 days to keep our home, and we did. I have countless stories like this where the pressure was off the charts, the stakes were all or nothing, the hours worked were at break-neck speed, but it was always worth it because I knew where I was going. Strategically working toward your goal makes hard work make sense.

STRATEGICALLY WORKING TOWARD YOUR GOAL MAKES
HARD WORK MAKE SENSE.

===

Andre Vicario

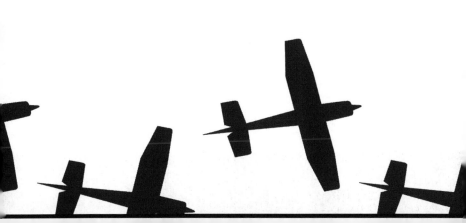

These are the times when you reflect and realize how much you have grown, how much you have sacrificed, and ultimately realizing anything is possible when you are committed.

Chapter 6: Reflect

Is there any area in your life that you feel like you are working hard without a strategic plan?

If you answered yes, write down which areas and set goals to make working that hard worth it.

_____

_____

_____

_____

Identify who can help you create a strategic plan to meet your goals and set the appointment.

_____

_____

_____

_____

*Examples: Financial Advisor, Business coach, Marketing strategist, Personal trainer, Counselor, etc. If you don't have the economic resources, read books, listen to podcasts or find a person you may respect and admire who is in your mind successful.

CHAPTER 7

START WHERE YOU ARE

Chapter 7:
Start Where You Are

The power generated from breaking the mold of mindsets that have held you back, surrounding yourself with people that go all-in on life, expanding your vision, setting a clear target, and strategically working hard is unbeatable. You feel possibility coursing through your veins, and opportunities are suddenly detectable everywhere; you realize you can change your life for the better as long as you take necessary action. Then you wake up the next day, and the sun rises like it always does, and you just want to fast forward to the part where everything worked out, and you have accomplished all you set out to do. This is the exact moment that matters most; the actions and decisions you make will be the difference between winning and losing. This moment is when you will determine things must change going forward in order to have a different result by your actions. You will experience hardship or even total discouragement, but if you are serious about making a change, you must do it now for your dreams to become your reality. Most people will stop at this point and feel discouraged. There is no better place to start than exactly where you are now. The actions or inactions of today are everything when you are creating a better future. We all want the change without having to change a thing, and it doesn't work this way. When you see what's possible and start believing it's possible for you specifically, it feels so exciting, even intoxicating. Still, if you don't connect the gravity of your smallest actions to your ultimate goals, which may be ten years away, you won't take them. The most successful people are crystal clear on this, set the long-term goal first, reverse engineer it back to today, and then relentlessly move forward. Author, Steven Covey says it best in his book The 7 Habits of Highly Effective People, 'Begin With The End In Mind.' If you have been pre-conditioned to live paycheck to paycheck, and aren't taking incremental action toward a long-term goal, this will be an adjustment for you.

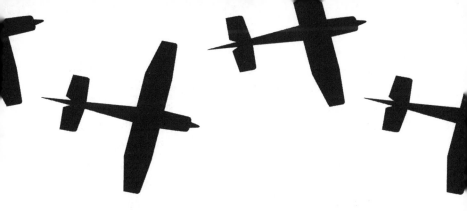

I HAVE NOT MET A PERSON YET WHO HAD A BIG VISION,
MADE A PLAN, TOOK ACTION, HIT THE GOAL,
BECAME FINANCIALLY FREE, AND REGRETTED IT.

Andre Vicario

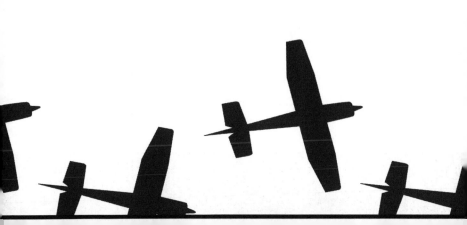

You start right where you are with whatever you have. I'm going to use an arbitrary example to put this in perspective. If you know you don't want to work after 50 years old and desire no less than $150,000 of passive income each year for the rest of your life, then you must find the right person to sit with you and make the plan. It may require you to invest $750 per month for 20 years if your 30 years old (again, I'm just making up numbers right now). If you knew for a fact that in 20 years, you will have an extra $150,000 coming to you annually for the rest of your life and it's going to happen by you investing $750 starting this month, and you are currently living paycheck to paycheck then it's time to get strategic and make it happen. How can you make an extra $187.50 per week to hit this goal of investing $750 per month? This may look like some part-time work two nights a week, starting a consulting business on the side, getting a job in sales, hitting larger commission goals, selling products online, getting your real estate license, and selling homes on the weekend. I literally can think of a thousand ways off the top of my head, and all of them are very doable. People often look at taking action to hit long-term goals as a sacrifice they aren't willing to make right now, but that doesn't make sense. We want the baby without the labor pains; it's just not reality. When we refuse to take today's actions to create a financially independent future, we sacrifice our peace and happiness now and later. Unless you are one of those rare souls who can live like a monk, happily with very little, or can't wait to work hard for the rest of your life only to find that you can't take your family on a single stress-free vacation, then you need to make a plan for your money. I have not met a person yet who had a big vision, made a plan, took action, hit the goal, became financially free, and regretted it. The only people I have met filled with regret are people who refused to make the necessary changes for a big beautiful life. Those people stay victimized by a poor mindset, and they refuse to change.

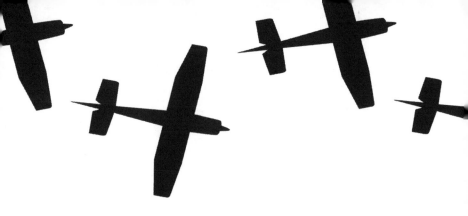

IF YOU ARE WILLING TO DO STRATEGIC HARD WORK TODAY,
YOU WILL HAVE WHATEVER SUCCESS YOU DESIRE TOMORROW
AND CAN MAKE WHATEVER DREAM YOU CHOOSE REALITY.

Andre Vicario

If you are willing to do strategic hard work today, you will have whatever success you desire tomorrow and can make whatever dream you choose reality. If you are willing to learn and ready to take action, then you cannot lose.

Chapter 7: Reflect

What changes have you been unwilling to make, yet deep down, you know your future self would thank you for?

_____

_____

_____

What do you believe is stopping you from making these changes?

_____

_____

_____

Create a list of the things you know you should do but have not started. Be truthful with yourself and write reasons for not doing these things.

_____

_____

_____

Once you have identified your list and have a better understanding of why you have not followed through, you must ask the question, "What would my life look like once I do these things I just don't want to do?"

_____

_____

_____

CHAPTER 8

REDEFINING WHAT'S POSSIBLE

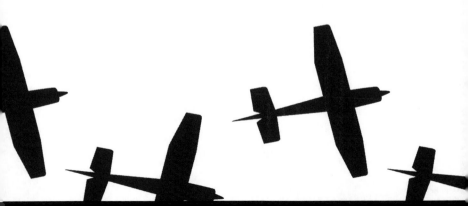

Chapter 8:
Redefining What's Possible

When you set your mind to make real change in your life, it can feel so confusing to find yourself tempted to stay the same. This is the cycle that halts possibilities. Why do we say we want to change course only to find ourselves clinging to the pieces of a life we aren't excited about repeatedly? I have seen it enough times to know that it happens to the very best of us on occasion, and it's a fight worth the effort to win.

Our comfort zone embodies what we already know, along with a sense of security about ourselves. If you have a lifetime of being worried about money and feeling like there's never enough, you're used to feeling and thinking this way even if you hate it. This becomes your normal. Everyone has a different sense of normal. We need to identify the new normal we aspire to achieve and begin to live it in every way, starting with changing your mindset. This is the beginning of redefining your "normal." If you are used to procrastinating, not making a plan, and sticking to it to create a better future, then you have become comfortable in the lack. The lure of familiarity is strong.

The only way out of this cycle of setting goals and staying stuck is by recognizing the pattern. Taking control of what comes over you when you start to make changes and intentionally keeping your plane on course despite your fear of uncertainty is the key.

You have to redefine what you believe is possible for yourself daily in your subconscious mind. Your conscious mind "saw the light," so to speak, made the goals, laid out the strategic plan of action, and has realized that changes must be made. Your subconscious mind, however, needs consistent reinforcement of the "new normal." The old you was pre-conditioned over a lifetime with a steady flow of messages from others and yourself about who you are and what is and isn't possible for your life. Habits were engrained to hold yourself to whatever life you have been living, but now you want to change some things. You will have to consistently remind yourself who you are choosing to become and make yourself take the new actions you have decided to take to set your life on a new trajectory.

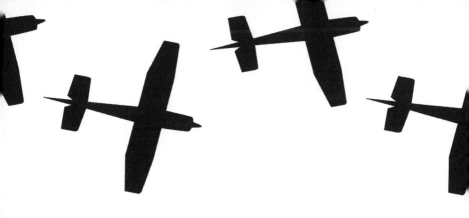

YOU HAVE TO REDEFINE WHAT YOU BELIEVE IS POSSIBLE FOR YOURSELF DAILY IN YOUR SUBCONSCIOUS MIND.

==

Andre Vicario

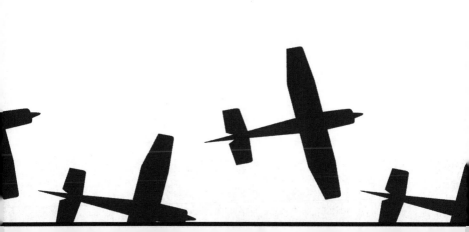

This work is conscious, intentional, and daily. You have to be strong enough to commit to the new you and manage the fear of uncertainty.

The old you might have felt stuck and frustrated, but you felt certainty and security. You knew who you were and what to expect. Your comfort zone is the place where nothing is challenged, questioned, or growing. The comfort zone is the land of the known. You know every twist and turn there. You expect not to have enough money and stress about it. You expect to feel like you're lost and frustrated. You're used to feeling like you don't know what to do to change things. You know exactly what your comfort zone is, and everything you desire that you don't currently have is outside of it. It's hard to leave a place that has become your home, even if you're miserable there.

THERE IS NOTHING STRONGER THAN THE HUMAN SPIRIT.

===

Andre Vicario

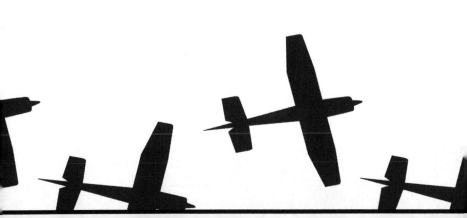

If you don't recognize what is going on inside you, it's easy to slip back into the old mold. You might find yourself running the same old programs in your mind about how you can't change and why your plan won't work, not to sabotage yourself but to feel normal and safe. You're not weak for wanting to feel secure-you're human. That said, because you're human, I know you have unlimited potential, and there is nothing stronger than the human spirit. You have made it this far, and you can shift your course with intention and vigilance today to hit your goals. When you become aware of the patterns you run in your mind that are holding you back, they lose their power. The only reason they have had any power in the first place is that they were allowed to run by you simply because you didn't know they existed. Your mind is in your house; you are in charge, nothing gets to happen in there without you allowing it. Fear of change is the most likely reason for staying the same. Why do we fear change so much? Getting out of our comfort zone is extremely challenging when we think about it. Make a task list, scratch things off once completed, and don't stop until each one is crossed off the list. By doing this one little thing, you will find accomplishments all around you. Now build on your list and turn them into a list of dreams, read them daily and let them be your North Star. Keep reviewing until you start on the journey to change your normal to the one you have long desired.

To help your subconscious mind fall in line with your new goals, you will have to confront the limiting beliefs that pop up, the limiting beliefs from your old normal.

Over time, those old limiting beliefs will eventually disappear, and your new normal beliefs will be what's left.

Chapter 8: Reflect

Take a minute to do this exercise so you can become very clear on the beliefs of your old normal and your new normal so you can create a different outcome:

Old Normal Beliefs	New Normal Beliefs
• I don't have enough money to get ahead.	• I have a plan that I'm sticking to that will always ensure I have plenty of money. Stick to the plan.
•	•
•	•

I guarantee you haven't even scratched the surface of what's possible for you yet. Come back to these new beliefs every morning when you wake up and each night before you fall asleep. You are your greatest source of influence in your life. The buck stops with you. Whether you think you can or can't, you're right. - Henry Ford

CHAPTER 9

MAKE YOUR MARK

Chapter 9:
Make Your Mark

How do you want to be remembered? One of the most noticeable side effects of living only for the short term is leaving your legacy to chance. Legacy is what lives on from you after your gone. By technical definition, legacy is an amount of money or property left to someone in a will. It's not uncommon for people not to want to think about their legacy because to think about it means you have to acknowledge that you don't have forever. Thinking about legacy brings up questions in us surrounding our choices and sometimes forces us to confront we aren't even close to leaving the kind of legacy behind we'd be proud of. Concerns about your legacy risk being ushered off into the waiting room of our mind that is reserved for topics that fall under "someday and later."

Sometimes, some things can be taken care of later or someday, like washing your car, ordering something online, or watching a movie. Basically, anything that requires zero preparation or planning can hang out in "someday or later." But if it matters to you at all and the goal fundamentally cannot be accomplished without time, a plan, or both, it cannot wait safely in "someday or later"; it needs to be moved into the "now" room.

Deep down, we know this to be true even if it's hard to tell yourself: If I don't start this today with a plan, it's *never* going to happen. If it's going to be, it's up to me, take ownership in the decisions you make and fight for the desired outcome.

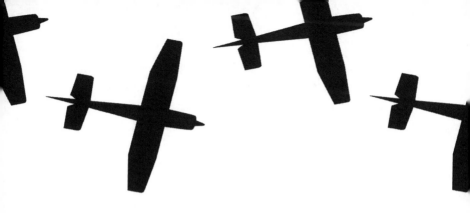

TAKE OWNERSHIP IN THE DECISIONS YOU MAKE AND FIGHT
FOR THE DESIRED OUTCOME.

===

Andre Vicario

If you want to lose 30lbs in the next six months for a vacation you have planned, you know you can't wait to take action because it requires time and effort no matter which way you spin it. If one week before your departure date, you wake up and realize you didn't lose a single pound, that's that. You can still go on the trip, but you're going to have to go just as you are and let the goal go. In truth, you can remake the plan and try again on the next round. It's frustrating, but it's not the end of the world. In truth, health and weight loss is a great place to start to change as it requires commitment and self-discipline, just like changing your mindset. I lost 35 pounds in two months and have not gained any of it back. I struggled with this for years. My tailor would ask, "Are we taking them in or out?" I had to fully commit to a healthier life, so it was time. What made it different this last time? I announced my goal to everyone. I had to follow through, or I would not have any credibility. I struggled daily but had a vision of myself being healthier and more fit to be working the long hours I do. Legacy takes follow-through.

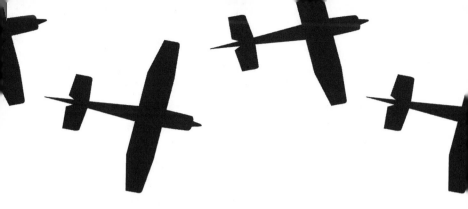

LEGACY TAKES FOLLOW-THROUGH.

Andre Vicario

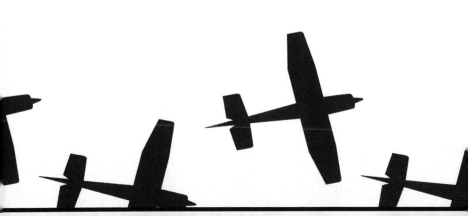

Legacy takes follow-through, no matter how uncomfortable it is to think about, legacy can't be half-assed, and it requires time and effort. I don't know where you are in the 80-100 year human life span, but I know that none of us truly do. I imagine one of the worst feelings would be to come to the end and see that you didn't do your best and everything still left in "someday or later" is moving to "never." I would rather cope with the uncomfortable feelings of long-term planning and get on track than cope with feeling like I failed with no time to fix it.

I had a conversation with my brother four months before his passing, and it's one I will never forget. He finally acknowledged I am living my life and enjoying it. He saved and had a bucket list with items still in it. He used to belittle me for how I lived and spent money. On this day, he was proud of how I live and happy I am buying the things I aspire to have. It took him being terminal to realize this. Don't wait for this moment; live your best life now. It takes the same effort to live an ordinary life as it does to live an extraordinary life once you combine passion and purpose. This is the true essence of living an abundant life. James Dean once said, "Dream as if you'll live forever. Live as if you'll die today."

I want to be remembered for how much I loved people, how hard I tried to help others, how I loved my wife and sons and did everything in my power to make life better for them. I want to leave behind a legacy that lives on through my sons and someday grandchildren. I want to leave behind wealth that will carry through generations. I want my team and my clients to carry forward everything I fought for so they can have more too. I want to leave behind a message and blueprints to living up to your full potential and squeeze every last drop out of living.

I am on track now to make sure this is my legacy. I take action every day towards all of this. If I waited until the last minute, I have no idea what I would have been leaving behind.

I work on my relationships every day. I connect with my family, team, company, and clients every day, ensuring everyone is taken care of. I make financial decisions every day to ensure that I can contribute to generations. I am taking care of my health every day to make sure I am here as long as possible. Legacy is a long-term goal, and when you realize this, it brings more meaning to life each day.

Chapter 9: Reflect

I want you to write down the legacy you would like to leave, then evaluate what changes you need to make to get yourself on track. If you found out today you are terminal and had only six months to live, would you have urgency to do the things you want to do but haven't yet? Remember, whatever changes you decide on need to begin now in the short-term. Do not leave this to chance.

Your Desired Legacy	Your Current Legacy	Changes You Must Make
	*If today was your last day, what is your legacy as of now?	

CHAPTER 10

CREATING IMPACT

Chapter 10:
Creating Impact

One of the best ways to stay out of your comfort zone and create a life you are genuinely proud of is to make it bigger than you. Focus on creating impact. When you know you are showing up every day because you have a plan and your plan will make you and your family's lives better, you will have a more challenging time getting in your own way. There are days when I am exhausted with at least 100 things coming at me from every direction that all need my attention, and it would be easy for me to want to shut down, but I don't. I understand that I am making an impact on far more people than just me. It started years ago with just wanting to prove to myself   that I could be the man I wanted to be, then it grew much bigger than me.

The first person you impact is yourself. We have talked about the role your thinking plays in the life you create around you. When you're exposing yourself to people who challenge you to be your best that you can learn from, you are impacting your life. When you choose to take actions that line up with an accurate vision of what you want, you impact yourself. When you vigilantly replace old limiting beliefs with newly expanded beliefs, you are impacting yourself. When you get in your corner and fight for the best version of yourself, a ripple effect begins to start moving out from you.

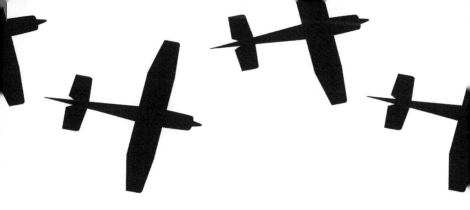

IMPACTING YOURSELF GIVES YOU THE STRENGTH
AND COURAGE TO IMPACT OTHERS INTENTIONALLY.

Andre Vicario

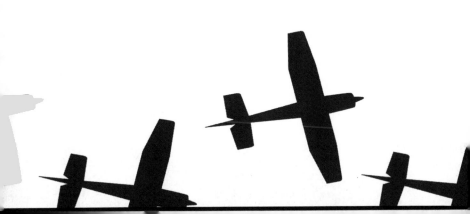

Impacting yourself gives you the strength and courage to impact others intentionally. Creating impact reminds me of the structure of a tree. The roots of the tree represent your mindset and what is happening inside of you. The trunk represents all of the actions you take based on your mindset, and the top of the tree represents your impact on the world.

With a strong nourished mindset, the roots grow deep and can support something massive. Strategically working hard on your mindset can create an enormous, solid trunk. With deep roots and a strong trunk, the top of the tree can grow as large as the base can withstand. Growth Mindset + Action = Impact.

GROWTH MINDSET + ACTION = IMPACT

===

Andre Vicario

Any insecurity you might have about yourself gets overshadowed when focusing on creating an impact. Attach your goals to your cause. What matters most to you, and how do you want to contribute? In the beginning, taking care of Kim and our boys was my primary cause. Eventually, helping my clients and the companies I worked for became part of my cause. Retiring my parents became part of my cause. Backing my sons as men and their futures is part of my cause. Expanding ModFinancial to help change the financial lives for as many people as possible become part of my cause.

Attaching what you do to what matters most to you gives you a superpower. Again, purpose and passion make you unstoppable. Combine this with a noble purpose, one which helps others, is even better and more inspiring. You will be able to run through brick walls if necessary, and this creates an impact.

Chapter 10: Reflect

Take a minute to think about the areas you want to impact.

What matters most to you?

_____

_____

_____

_____

What is important to you enough to make you want to make a difference?

_____

_____

_____

_____

What can you start doing today, even if it's small, to take action on creating impact?

_____

_____

_____

_____

What is the impact I am currently making?	What is the impact I want to make?
*	*

Impact takes perseverance. It's ordinary to only think about your immediate family and friends closest to you. If you want extraordinary, start thinking about your impact on the world.

CHAPTER 11

THE CULTURE WITHIN

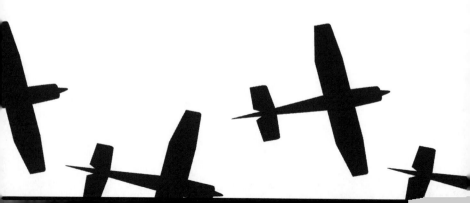

Chapter 11:
The Culture Within

I used to have a hard time connecting with others. I could be in a room full of people and still feel alone. To look at me, no one would ever guess that I felt disconnected. I built great relationships professionally and genuinely invested in my amazing wife and boys, but this guard I didn't even know I had until later in life remained. Feeling so out of place as a child and young man, I just felt compelled always to prove myself. As I shared before, this sense of feeling inadequate lingered, and from that stemmed this tough exterior that would ensure I was never found out. I made sure I appeared unshaken by anything, but it also kept me feeling isolated.

Then I discovered something that changed me forever and continues to evolve me and my connection to others daily.

I started to let my guard down, and it unleashed a new level of freedom and success I had no idea I was even missing out on. I have been leading teams since my early 20's, and we always did well. I would give 110%, making sure we always hit our goals and progressed. This contributed to how and why I moved so quickly up the proverbial ladder anywhere I went. Wins never fully felt like wins unless we were all moving forward. If my clients or team members weren't succeeding, then I felt like I wasn't either. I share this because it helped me realize something critical I had never seen in myself before; everything I do comes from a place of love. How hard I've pushed myself and others to be their best, the constant accountability and training inside my company, worrying about how everyone is doing, it wasn't coming from being tough on people or even about the success. It was my way of trying to help as many people as possible. Realizing this about myself had a profound effect on me. It gave me the green light that it was ok for me to let people in. I realized it was never about my goals alone; it had always been about the people hitting their goals too. I was given the book The Servant by James C. Hunter years ago and have read it at least 20 times since. It echoed to me what I believed was true leadership. You share power, put the needs of employees and people first, and help others reach their full potential. In short, the servant leader exists to serve the people, not the people who exist to serve the leader. When I realized my primary driver in every move I make is coming from love, it made me realize it might not only be good for me to start letting my guard down, but it could bring in something even better. Helping people was great but feeling connected to them amplified everything tenfold. It created a culture on the inside of me that became the culture I created around me.

As a pilot, I am in charge of all passengers' safety and setting the correct flight coordinates to our desired destination. I have had to learn to navigate turbulence, stay calm through assessment and keep us on our predetermined flight path despite atmospheric pressures changing beyond my control. I have also learned to know when it's time to move from autopilot to manual override and set new coordinates when necessary. I know how to listen to ground control and take a go-around for an alternative safe approach to landing if something is off with the original plan. Through all of my years in aviation, I have seen the cross-over from the pilot in me to my company and its culture. We fly together safely to our destinations with smooth landings and get through any turbulence along the way.

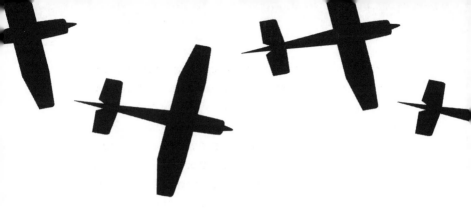

OUR EXTERNAL CULTURE IS A REFLECTION
OF OUR INTERNAL CULTURE.

Andre Vicario

Our external culture is a reflection of our internal culture. Culture is created, whether we are intentional about it or not, created in our homes, with our friends, and professionally. Culture can be considered the growth of a group identity and its collective beliefs, behaviors, achievements, etc. There are hundreds of people on my team today, and our company culture is intentionally cultivated daily by all of us. As a person in a place of leadership, I have the opportunity to intentionally co-create the culture that my team experiences and the experience of our clients.

Our culture is built on a growth mindset and a desire to genuinely help others succeed. Every team member practices what they preach. They set personal goals and take full responsibility for achieving them. We help our clients reach their personal and family goals not the companies goals or any third party. We believe in creating lives that we can all be proud of and are committed to doing whatever it takes to rise together. We celebrate each others' wins and challenge each other to learn and grow stronger if we are missing the mark. This is the culture I have aspired to with my family and my friends, commitment to our personal best, accountability when we know we can do better, and being there for each other through turbulence and clear skies. I believe in transparency and authenticity; I'm the same person in private as I am in public. We all go through it, hell I've been through all of it, and it's never been about being perfect. It's about committing to the best version of myself so I can give the best I've got to this world. Yes, I hold people accountable to their full potential because I believe that's what you do when you really care about people. I believe in a culture that cultivates dreams taking flight. The people that have come along side me personally and professionally want the same. The culture we have created is a direct reflection of our mindset, the culture within.

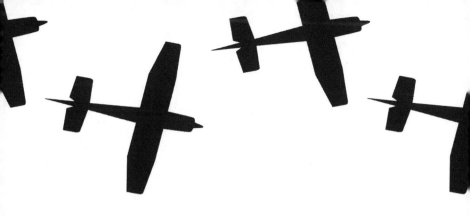

COMMIT TO THE BEST VERSION OF YOURSELF SO
YOU CAN GIVE THE BEST YOU'VE GOT TO THIS WORLD.

Andre Vicario

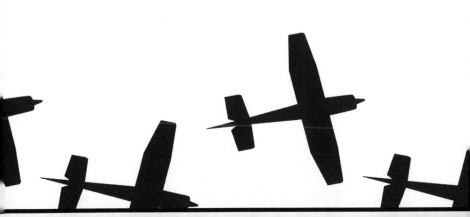

Chapter 11: Reflect

What kind of culture are you creating?

If you are not happy with the culture you are creating, list 5 actions you could do to improve it.

_____

_____

_____

_____

_____

_____

_____

CHAPTER 12

COMMITTED VS. INTERESTED

Chapter 12:
Committed Vs. Interested

It is common to be interested in success. It is uncommon to be committed. When someone tells me they want to be successful, my first question is, "Are you committed or interested?" It's important to know the difference because only one will bring you success, and if you haven't guessed, being interested isn't it.

When we are interested in something, it can be a hobby, something we do for fun, or when we feel like it in our free time. Being interested does not require relentless fortitude that commitment does. Interest requires curiosity or casual concern, and there is nothing wrong with being interested in success or anything else for that matter. The only time interest becomes a problem is when you set important goals based on interest.

When I set a goal, I know I have to be committed to the goal, or I may as well not waste my time. Commitment has an entirely different energy than interest. Commitment is a pledge or dedication to seeing the goal through. Think about all that we have covered about limiting beliefs, fear of uncertainty, and the challenges that arise internally when we expand our vision and begin making changes. Left unchecked, we will forever be interested in change and the benefits of the results, but we will never make it past our self-proclaimed limitations without commitment to it.

Every time I commit to a new goal, I already know I am leaving my comfort zone behind. I expect to deal with all of the feelings of uncertainty that could only be silenced by going backward, back to my comfort zone, but because of my commitment, I stay the course at all cost.

Years ago, I walked into an art gallery with my family, interested in one particular artist's work. Every guest that walked in was immediately offered champaign and welcomed. I was there with my mom and boys for nearly 20 minutes, and no one had spoken a word to us. I didn't think much of it, and I had already found the pieces I wanted to buy when my mom needed to use the restroom. I watched as she asked one of the welcoming staff where the restroom was, and they told her there was one at a convenience store up the street. I looked across the room and saw guests going in and out of the restroom located inside the art gallery. I looked at my son as his face filled with so much anger. His eyes were burning. I knew what he felt because it had happened to me so many times. I walked up to the sales associate, who directed my mom to a restroom up the street and asked if he directed all of his guests to an offsite restroom. He looked slightly caught off guard but maintained a very complacent tone. Before he could answer, I asked if he offered champaign to all of the guests or just a select few? He showed no remorse as he said, "I'm sorry I didn't see you come in." I said that it was fine and let him know what pieces I was purchasing so we could leave. He responded by asking me if I was aware of how much the pieces cost. Needless to say, I was angry, but I stayed calm and let him know he would be offering me 20% off for the way he treated my family, and I was deducting his commission from the ticket as well. He realized the mistake he had made, and I bought the art I wanted.

Am I interested in creating an incredible life for my family and me, or am I committed? If I were interested, the way I have been treated would have broken me before I ever got started, and if the early years didn't take me out of the game, incidences like the Art Gallery would have in the end. But no, I have never let any of it stop me. I don't need to scream and fight about it. I stay focused on the final destination and the landing. I know who I am and what I want, and I am committed to doing whatever it takes to bring me and everyone around me up. I wasn't interested in building a successful company, my interest would have vanished the minute Kim and I sold every fund and asset we had to start it with no guarantee. I wasn't interested in taking care of my wife and sons; interest would have gotten me as far as paycheck to paycheck. I am not interested in creating financial freedom for myself and others; I am committed every day to literally thousands of moving parts that keep every piece moving forward successfully.

STAY FOCUSED ON THE FINAL DESTINATION AND THE LANDING.

Andre Vicario

People are usually committed until they meet resistance, then they becomes interested. They talk themselves into believing its not as important as they once thought. This is the very moment we let our dreams go, lack of commitment. We live in a commitment phobic society, people are afraid to be committed. Being committed means you must stay the course no matter what, this creates fear for most and therefore they relent and now become interested. The key to any level of happiness or success is the discipline to commitment. It does take discipline to be happy and to be successful, you must be committed to it with discipline. Commitment takes guts and is a full-contact sport. Either I'm all in, or I'm not committed; I'm just interested.

If you've realized you need a bigger vision and you are ready to set real goals, if you are committed, you will succeed. Implementation and execution are a product of the commitment you have made in your mind. The blueprints already exist to show you exactly how to build whatever vision you have. The road map to your financial success can be easily created to match your needs, wants, and desires. The "how" was never the obstacle that stopped anyone from building their American Dream and breaking free of the mold of somebody else's limitations. You are the hero in your own story, and you can rewrite any part of it, harness its power and set yourself free.

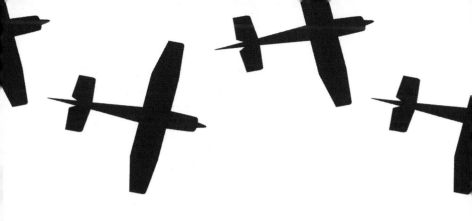

YOU ARE THE HERO IN YOUR OWN STORY,
AND YOU CAN REWRITE ANY PART OF IT.

Andre Vicario

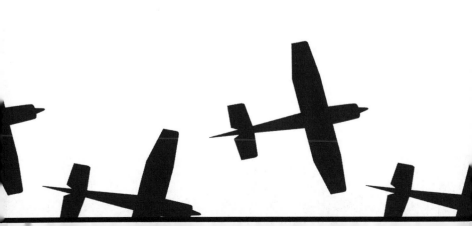

As I look out to the horizon, I see a world of possibility, filled with those of you courageous enough to build greatness together. When I'm out there kicking ass— I know you will be too.

Roger. Wilco. Out